OMAD

Intermittent Fasting:

Guide to Losing Fat, Increasing your Spirituality and Getting More Work Done

monetary loss due to the information herein, either directly or indirectly.

Legal Notice:

This book is copyright protected. This is only for personal use. You cannot amend, distribute, sell, use, quote or paraphrase any part of the content within this book without the consent of the author.

Disclaimer Notice:

Please note the information contained within this document is for educational and entertainment purposes only. Every attempt has been made to provide accurate, up to date and complete, reliable information. No warranties of any kind are expressed or implied. Readers acknowledge that the author is not engaging in the rendering of legal, financial, medical or professional advice. The content of this book has been derived from various sources. Please consult a licensed professional before attempting any techniques outlined in this book.

By reading this document, the reader agrees that under no circumstances is the author responsible for any losses, direct or indirect, which are incurred as a result of the use of information contained within this document, including, but not limited to, —errors, omissions, or inaccuracies.

Table of Contents

Introduction

I want to thank you for choosing this book, '*One Meal a Day Intermittent Fasting - Guide to Losing Fat, Increasing your Spirituality and Getting More Work Done.*'

Are you looking for a diet that will help you lose weight and improve your health? Do you want a diet that doesn't insist on counting calories? Imagine if you could achieve your fitness and weight loss goals without counting calories! That does sound quite wonderful, doesn't it? If your answer is yes, then intermittent fasting is the diet that you were searching for.

The concept of fasting is not a new one and it has been around since time immemorial. People tend to fast for medical, health or even spiritual reasons. Intermittent fasting is a simple dieting protocol that alternates between periods of fasting and eating.

In this book, you will learn about the One Meal a Day protocol of intermittent fasting. You will also read about the basics of intermittent fasting, the changes that take place in your body while fasting, different methods of intermittent fasting, the benefits it offers, tips for weight loss and the spirituality of fasting. Apart from this, you will also learn about the different ways in which this diet improves your overall productivity so that you can get more work done! Also, the success stories given in this book will inspire you to try this diet for yourself.

So, if you are ready to learn more about this wonderful diet that can turn your life around, then let us get started right away!

Chapter One: What is OMAD and Intermittent Fasting?

Intermittent fasting is a simple concept - you are free to eat almost anything that you want for a specific period of time and then you need to fast for a while until it is time to eat again. During the fasting period, you are free to eat anything that doesn't have any calories in it. Intermittent fasting is a simple concept and you can find a method that will suit your personal needs.

Unlike other forms of traditional dieting, the idea of fasting is quite unambiguous and easy to understand. Did you know that most of us tend to fast from time to time anyway? Usually, we tend to fast without thinking about it, and it isn't a conscious decision. When you think about it, did you ever skip a meal in a day? If you did, then you were following an intermittent fasting protocol. You will learn about the different methods of intermittent fasting in the coming chapters.

Our caveman ancestors were predominantly hunters and gatherers. So, if they needed to eat, they had to hunt or search for food in nature. It meant that they used to fast until they found some form of nourishment. Then agriculture came along, and it led to the creation of human civilization. Whenever there was scarcity of food or whenever the seasons changed, fasting was the norm of life. It was a common practice to maintain stores of grain and meat in the cities and castles to survive harsh winters. Before the advent of agriculture, a shortage of rainfall meant a spell of famine and people used to fast to ensure that their food supplies would last them longer. Sufficient rain was a precondition to meet the necessary grain requirement.

Religions cropped up with the civilizations. Religions grew when people started to live in close quarters and started to share similar beliefs. Most of these religions tended to prescribe some form of fasting. In Hinduism, fasting is known as Vaasa and is said to be a form of penance. Islam prescribes fasting during the holy month of Ramadan. A similar practice exists in Judaism and is known as Yom Kippur. Even Christianity prescribes fasting before Easter.

Technology and innovation played a major role in the evolution of human beings.
Industrialization completely revolutionized the food industry. It introduced the concept of mass production of food products. It meant that the markets are flooded with food products all the

time. Apart from this, the way human beings view and consume food has also undergone a massive overhaul. The world that humans live in has changed a lot, but the human body didn't get an opportunity to acclimatize itself to the changes that were brought about by industrialization and the advent of agriculture. All this does signify the growth of the human race, but it also meant the introduction of a variety of health problems that humans were not used to. The practice of intermittent fasting can be traced back centuries. Even though it is an old practice, humans have just started to fully understand and appreciate the different benefits this diet provides. Whenever you are fasting, you tend to give your body a chance to cleanse itself from within. Not just cleanse, but even regenerate and repair itself from within.

While you are fasting, your body gets an opportunity to burn all the excess fat that it keeps stored within. Humans have evolved in such a manner that it is quite safe to fast, and there are no risks involved in fasting. The body fat stored in the cells is the reserve of food that the body stores away for a rainy day. When you don't consume any food, your body merely reaches into its internal stores to provide energy.

It is the law of nature that there needs to be balance in all aspects of life. The Chinese concept of yin and yang is quite practical and these rules apply to eating and fasting too. Eating and fasting are the two sides of a single coin. Fasting is the flipside of eating so when you don't eat, you are fasting. Whenever you eat something, it leads to the accumulation of energy that your body doesn't use immediately. A portion of all that you eat is stored away for later use. Insulin, a hormone that is secreted by pancreas is responsible for storing energy. Whenever you eat something, there is a spike of insulin in your body. Insulin helps the body store energy in two different ways. The sugars are linked into long chains known as glycogen and the rest is stored in the liver.

There is only so much fat that the liver can hold onto so, the rest is sent to different cells in the body in the form of fat. Liver stores some fat and the rest is safely stowed away in different cells. There is no limit to the amount of fat that the body can churn out. There are two forms of energy that are present in the body. One of these forms is easily accessible but has a limited storage space and is known as glycogen. The other form of energy is harder to reach into and has an unlimited storage space, which is known as body fat.

When you don't eat anything, your body reverses this process. There will be a decline in the level of insulin and it encourages your body to dip into its stores of fat. Once your body accesses this fat, it starts to burn it to provide energy. Glycogen is the most easily attainable source of energy in the body. It is quite easy to break the glycogen molecules down to provide energy. The energy that's produced like this can sustain your body for 24 hours or even longer. After your body exhausts its reserves of glucose, it starts to burn fat to provide energy.

Your body will continue to do this only when you are eating or fasting. Either your body is burning energy or it is storing energy. Only one of these processes can take place at a time. If there is a balance between when you eat and fast, then it doesn't lead to any weight gain. Over a period, you will start to put on weight if you don't give your body the time it needs to burn the food that it is storing within. To restore the quintessential balance in your body, you need to give it plenty of time to burn the stored food for energy. If you want to accomplish this, then intermittent fasting is necessary. In fact, this is precisely how our bodies are designed by nature. Intermittent fasting helps restore this balance.

Circadian Rhythm and Intermittent Fasting

Like all the other organisms on this Earth, even human beings have an internal circadian clock that ensures that all the physiological processes are being performed at the right time. The circadian rhythm is switched on all day long and it has an effect on the biology as well as the behavior of human beings.

Any disruption in the circadian rhythm will have a negative effect on the metabolism and it causes various metabolic dysfunctions like obesity, diabetes and a host of cardiovascular problems. The primary factor that regulates the circadian rhythm is the signal to feed. It is responsible for the functioning of all the metabolic, physiological and behavioral pathways in the body. In turn, all these different pathways are responsible to ensure that your body performs optimally. Apart from this, the circadian rhythm also ensures that your body is healthy. A form of behavioral intervention is necessary to regulate the circadian rhythm in the body. Yes, you guessed it right! The behavioral intervention that I am talking about is intermittent fasting. Intermittent fasting helps streamline the circadian rhythm. All this helps to improve the gene expression and leads to an overall improvement in your body's health as well as metabolism.

Gut Microbiome and Intermittent Fasting

The gastrointestinal tract is responsible for regulating various processes within your body. In other words, your gut is responsible for regulating various physiological and biochemical functions going on in your body. For instance, did you know that the metabolic reaction to glucose as well as blood flow tend to be higher during the day than at night? Even a slight fluctuation in the circadian rhythm tends to impair your metabolism and it increases the risk factor of different chronic health problems. The microbiome that's present in the gut is known as the second brain. It is referred to as such because it exerts certain control over your overall metabolism and physiology. Intermittent fasting tends to have a positive effect on the gut microbiome. It tends to make the gut less permeable, reduces the chances of systemic inflammation and improves the balance of energy.

Lifestyle Behavior and Intermittent Fasting

Intermittent fasting also helps change different behaviors important for health like the sleep cycle, calorie consumption and energy usage. Therefore, it doesn't come as a surprise that any imbalance in these three is the primary reason for any health concern. You will learn more about the different benefits of intermittent fasting in the coming chapters.

Different Methods of Fasting

16/8 method

The 16/8 method is one of the easiest intermittent fasting protocols there is. We are all effectively fasting while asleep and this method is simply an extension of that fasting period. Most of us tend to skip our breakfast and tend to have our first meal after 12 noon. Well, in this method of fasting, you simply have to make sure that your eating window doesn't exceed 8 hours. In this process, an individual is required to fast for 16 hours in a day. The eating window is restricted to 8 hours. Two regular or three small meals can be squeezed into this period. This method is quite simple to follow. It can be something as simple as skipping breakfast or not munching on anything after dinner. For instance, you can make sure that the last meal that you have is at 8 in the evening. Make sure that you don't eat anything until 12 noon the following day. It provides you with a fasting window of about 16 hours. It has been observed that it would be better if women fast for a shorter duration of time and don't let their fasting period go beyond 14-15 hours. For those who feel hungry in the morning and are used to having breakfast every day, this can be hard initially. However, if you were already used to skipping breakfast, then it will be easy. You can have water, coffee and other beverages that don't have many calories in them while you are fasting. If you are just getting started with intermittent fasting, then this is the fasting protocol that you must consider.

5:2 Diet

If the idea of fasting daily doesn't appeal to you, then you can follow the 5:2 dieting protocol. While following this diet, the individual gets to eat regularly on five days of the week and restricts the calorie intake to 500-600 calories on the other two days of the week. This diet is referred to as the Fast diet. On the two fasting days, it is recommended that women must have 500 calories and men can consume 600 calories.

For instance, you get to eat regularly on all days except the two days when you want to fast. On such days, you can eat two meals consisting of 250-300 calories each depending on your gender. This diet is suitable for all those who feel that they cannot fast for the whole day and who would like to eat a little something. 5:2 diet is a very simple diet. You have control over deciding the days on which you want to fast and the days on which you don't. If you don't like the idea of abstaining from eating, then this is well suited for you. The days when you are fasting, you can either stick to a strict diet or give yourself permission to have around 500 calories.

Eat-stop-Eat

This form of intermittent fasting requires the individual to fast for 24 hours, once or twice every week. You will need to fast for 24 hours consecutively on this diet. From dinner on one day until dinner the consecutive day, that will constitute 24 hours. For instance, you had your dinner at 7 p.m. on Monday, and you don't get to eat until 7 p.m. on Tuesday. This will be the 24 hours fasting window. You can also do this from breakfast on a given day until breakfast on the following day. You will just need to fast for 24 hours; you can select the timings according to your convenience. You cannot consume any solid food during this diet.

However, water, coffee and other beverages that don't have any calories in them can be safely consumed. If you are following this method because you want to lose weight, then in such a case you will need to eat regularly during your feeding window. You must eat the sort of food you are used to eating, had you not been fasting. The only problem with this method is that there happens to be a 24-hour fasting window and it might be difficult for a few people to follow. You don't have to start out with this necessarily. You can gradually progress from the 16-hour fasting model. The first stretch of the diet will not be hard; it is only toward the end that this diet gets a little complicated to follow. This is where discipline and motivation will come in handy.

If you keep yourself busy, then you won't have time to think about food or hunger. So, on the fasting days, make sure that you keep yourself busy or engaged. Plan your day so that you are indulging in activities that keep you occupied. You must have plenty of water. Not only will it keep your body thoroughly hydrated, but it will also leave you feeling full for longer. Make sure that you plan your week in such a manner that your fasting days don't clash with any other social obligations. Intermittent fasting protocols are quite convenient, and you don't have to compromise on your social life for the sake of this diet.

Alternate day fasting

As the name suggests, this diet is all about fasting on every alternate day. There are different variations of this diet. If you want, you can fast for 24-hours on every alternate day and then there are other variations that allow you to eat about 500 calories on every alternate day, and the others require you to observe a strict fast on every alternate day. Most of the lab studies that have been conducted to find the benefits of intermittent fasting have made use of some variation of this diet. A strict fast might sound rather severe and extreme. Depending upon your comfort level, you can adapt this diet to suit your needs.

It is advisable that beginners don't immediately jump to this method. With this method of fasting, be prepared to go to bed hungry a few times every week. This diet doesn't show any form of sustainability in the long run.

Warrior diet

This kind of fasting involves the consumption of small quantities of raw fruit and veggies during the day and then consuming a single hearty meal at night. Mostly, you will need to fast throughout the day, and then you get to feast at night. The feeding window extends to only 4 hours. This variation of the intermittent fasting diets was one of the first ones to be popular. While following this method of fasting, the food choices that you make must be quite similar to what you will have made had you been following the Paleo diet. You will need to consume foods that are unprocessed. You can eat anything that our cavemen ancestors will have consumed. If something looks like it was produced in a factory, you must certainly avoid it.

The Paleo diet is a high fat and a low carb diet, just like the ketogenic diet. The protocols of a Paleo diet can be successfully combined with the dieting protocols of an intermittent fast. For instance, if you are following the alternate day model of fasting, then on the days when you aren't fasting you must follow a Paleo diet. You just have to make sure that whenever you are eating, the food that you are consuming is Paleo-friendly. So, you cannot have any form of processed foods, starchy foods or carbs. By combining these two diets, you can reap the benefits of the Paleo diet and intermittent fasting as well.

Skipping meals spontaneously

Well, this is an obvious one and this form of intermittent fasting doesn't have a structured plan. You will simply have to skip meals spontaneously from time to time. Skip meals whenever you aren't hungry, or you are preoccupied with some work. If you aren't hungry, then don't eat. It is as simple as that. Just skip a meal whenever you feel like it. Then depending on how hungry you are you can have a hearty meal after that. However, you will need to make sure that the other meals that you are consuming are healthy. Skipping meals is not the same as starvation. Don't try to starve yourself, that's not what this method is about. By skipping meals when you aren't hungry, you are reducing the unnecessary calorie consumption. Your body knows what it needs and learn to listen to it. Eat only when you are hungry.

One Meal a Day Diet

The popularity of intermittent fasting is increasing every day. One method of IF that is steadily becoming quite popular is the One

Meal a Day diet also known as the OMAD diet. Abstaining from food helps modulate your body's performance and when you fast for prolonged periods, it has a positive effect on your body and mind.

The OMAD protocol is designed in such a manner that the fasting ratio you need to follow is 23:1. It means that your body will be effectively fasting for 23 hours and the eating window is restricted to one hour. If you want to burn fat, trigger weight loss, improve your mental clarity and reduce the time that you spend on food, then eating one meal a day is a brilliant idea.

The OMAD method oscillates between periods of eating and fasting. This method of fasting reduces the eating window more than the other diets. While following this dieting protocol, you need to make sure that you consume your daily calories within one meal and you fast for the rest of the day. OMAD helps you reap all the benefits of intermittent fasting and it simplifies your schedule as well. The ideal time to break your fast is between 4 and 7 p.m. When you do this, you give your body sufficient time to start digesting the food that you eat before you sleep.

From the perspective of evolution, humans aren't designed to eat three meals per day. As mentioned earlier, our ancestor's bodies were used to functioning optimally even when there was food scarcity. Intermittent fasting protocols like the OMAD tend to kickstart various cell functions in your body that are helpful to improve your overall health. It can be quite intimidating to get started with this method of dieting. There are three simple tips that you can follow to make the transition easier on yourself.

The first thing that you need to do is **slowly cut back on the carbs** that you consume. If you want to optimize the results of this diet and want the least amount of crankiness, then you must limit your carb intake. When you consume a lot of carbs, your body tends to create a stock of glycogen in the body. If there is always some glucose present in your body, then your body will not be able to shift into ketosis. Ketosis is essential to kickstart the process of burning fats. So, if you are trying to start this diet, then it is a good idea to start by slowly cutting back on your carb intake.

You need to **ease your body into getting used to this fasting protocol**. It can be quite difficult to go from eating three meals a day to just one meal a day. You need to ease the transition so that it doesn't feel like you are suffering. A simple way in which you can do this is by slowly getting your body used to the idea of eating fewer meals. So, if you are used to eating three meals per day and tend to snack in between the meals, then the first step is to eliminate all the snacks. Then you can slowly increase the time between the meals and cut down on the number of meals you eat. If you do this, it will be quite easy to follow this diet.

Another simple way in which you can make this diet easier on your body is to consume some caffeine. A morning cup of coffee (devoid of milk and sugar) will make you feel fuller for longer and will keep your hunger pangs at bay. You will learn more about the different tips that you can follow to manage your hunger in the coming chapters.

Chapter Two: Weight Loss

Your body tends to store energy in the form of fat cells. When you don't eat anything, there a couple of different changes that take place in your body that help your body access its energy reserves. There are a couple of changes that take place in the activity of your nervous system. Here are a couple of changes that take place in the metabolism of your body whenever you fast.

Insulin- The level of insulin increases whenever you eat. So, while you are fasting, the insulin levels in your body will decrease. A low level of insulin means that it is easier for your body to burn the fats that are stored within.

Human Growth Hormone - The human growth hormone or HGH level increases when you fast. This hormone is responsible for not just fat loss, but it also helps with muscle gain and it kick starts autophagy.

Noradrenaline - Norepinephrine or noradrenaline is sent to the fat cells by the nervous system to help break down the fat in the body and to free up the reserves of fatty acids to provide energy.

If you keep consuming food throughout the day, then it is unlikely that any of these changes will take place. Short-term fasting helps increase your body's ability to burn fats. So, a short-term fast like intermittent fasting induces several changes in your body that makes it easier to burn fat. It also reduces the production of insulin while increasing the production of the growth hormone and epinephrine to give a metabolic boost to your body.

Intermittent fasting helps you reduce your intake of calories and helps with weight loss. The primary reason why intermittent fasting is an effective weight loss technique is because it reduces your calorie intake. As such there is no calorie restrictions prescribed by this diet. All the different methods of intermittent fasting involve foregoing meals during the periods of fast. Unless you try to compensate for all this by eating more during the eating window, then you will certainly be consuming fewer calories than usual. Intermittent fasting can lead to significant weight loss if you carefully follow the protocols of this diet for at least three weeks. It isn't just fat loss that you will experience on this diet; you will also notice that you are losing fat from your abdominal region. The benefits of intermittent fasting are not restricted to just weight loss. This diet has a positive effect on your metabolic health and also helps prevent any chronic diseases.

You don't have to necessarily count calories while following any method of intermittent fasting, but you need to maintain a calorie deficit if you want to lose weight. Intermittent fasting helps reduce your calorie intake without setting up any calorie restrictions.

One of the side effects of a diet that helps you lose fat is that it also causes you to burn muscle while burning fat. When it comes to intermittent fasting, you will not be burning any muscle mass and, in fact, it helps you gain lean muscle mass. The reduction in muscle mass while on intermittent fasting is quite low when compared to a diet that prescribes continuous calorie restriction.

Apart from this, it is also easier to eat healthily while following this diet. The simplicity of this diet is the main reason for all the benefits it offers. You can select any method of intermittent fasting and you will notice that you are eating healthier meals than before. If you want to follow the OMAD protocol, then you can eat only one meal per day. If you can eat only one meal, then you need to make sure that the meal that you eat will fill you up so that you can go through the day without feeling hungry. The foods that will fill you up for longer are foods rich in protein and fiber. So, knowingly or unknowingly you will start to incorporate healthy foods into your diet. For instance, eating a bowl of lettuce will make you feel fuller for longer than a packet of chips. So, you will be making healthier food choices.

At the end of the day, intermittent fasting is a wonderful dieting protocol that you can follow to lose weight. The main reason for weight loss on this diet is the reduction in the intake of calories.

Chapter Three: Improved Health

Intermittent fasting is a wonderful dieting protocol that offers several health benefits. In this section, you will learn about the different ways in which this diet will improve your overall health.

Weight loss

One of the primary benefits of intermittent fasting is weight loss. Intermittent fasting oscillates between periods of eating and fasting. While fasting, your calorie intake reduces naturally and it helps you lose weight and maintain it as well. Apart from that, it also stops you from indulging in any form of mindless eating. Whenever you consume food, your body converts the food into glucose. The glucose that it needs immediately is converted into energy and the rest is stored within the body in the form of fat cells. Not all the food you consume is converted into energy. So, all the unused energy is stored as fat within your cells. When you start to skip meals, your body will reach into its internal stores of energy. Once your body starts to burn fats to provide energy it automatically kick starts the process of weight loss. Also, most of the fat is usually stored in the abdominal region. If you want to lose fat from your abdominal region, then this is the best diet for you.

Sleep

Obesity is rampant these days. In fact, it is a major health problem that humanity is suffering from. The primary cause of obesity apart from terrible lifestyle and food choices is the lack of sleep. Intermittent fasting regulates your circadian rhythm and it encourages better sleep cycle. When your body is sufficiently rested, it is capable of burning fats effectively. A good sleep cycle has several physiological benefits like an increase in your energy levels and an overall improvement in your mood.

Resistance to illnesses

Intermittent fasting assists in the growth as well as the regeneration of cells. Did you know that the human body has an internal mechanism for repairing all the damaged cells? Well, think of it as internal housekeeping that ensures that all the cells in your body are performing optimally. When you follow the protocols of intermittent fasting it improves the overall functioning of your cells. So, it directly helps improve the natural defense mechanism in your body and increases the resistance to diseases as well as illnesses.

A healthy heart

As mentioned in the previous chapter, intermittent fasting promotes weight loss. Burning up all the stored unnecessary fats in the body helps improve your cardiovascular health. The buildup of plaque in the blood vessels is referred to as atherosclerosis. Atherosclerosis occurs when fat deposits start building up in the blood vessels and it is the primary cause of different cardiovascular diseases. Endothelium is a thin lining present in the blood vessels and a dysfunction of this lining causes atherosclerosis. Obesity is one of the main reasons for the build-up of plaque in blood vessels. Stress, as well as inflammation, worsens this problem. Intermittent fasting helps reduce and remove the plaque deposits and helps tackle obesity. So, if you want to improve the health of your heart, then this is the best diet for you.

A healthy gut

Did you know that your gut is the home for several millions of microorganisms? These microorganisms are helpful and are essential for the optimal functioning of the digestive system. These microorganisms are known as microbiome. The gut microbiome is necessary for a healthy gut. A healthy digestive system helps with better absorption of food and improves the functioning of your stomach. So, a simple diet change can help you improve your gut's health.

Tackles diabetes

Diabetes is a terrible problem. In fact, it is right alongside with obesity as one of the leading health concerns these days. Diabetes is also a primary indicator for the risk in the increase of different cardiovascular diseases like heart attacks and strokes. When the level of glucose is alarmingly high in the bloodstream and there isn't sufficient insulin to process the glucose, it causes diabetes. When the body starts developing a resistance to insulin, it is quite difficult to regulate the sugar levels in the body. Intermittent fasting reduces the problem of insulin sensitivity and effectively helps tackle and manage diabetes.

Reduces inflammation

Whenever your body notices an internal problem, it powers up its natural defense mechanism - inflammation. Inflammation in moderate amounts is desirable and helpful. However, it doesn't mean that all forms of inflammation are good. Excess inflammation causes various health problems like arthritics, atherosclerosis and neurodegenerative disorders. Any inflammation of this form is known as chronic inflammation. Chronic inflammation is quite painful, and it can restrict your body's movements.

Promotes cell repair

When you start fasting, the cells in your body engage themselves in the process of waste removal. Waste removal refers to the process of breaking down dysfunctional cells and proteins. This process is known as autophagy and is quintessential for the upkeep of your body. Do you like accumulating waste in your home? Similarly, it is important to ensure that your body doesn't start collecting any toxic wastes. Autophagy is the natural way of getting rid of all unnecessary things from your body. Autophagy protects the neurons in your brain from any cell degeneration. It not only protects the neurons, but it also prevents them from excitotoxic stress. All this helps the brain replace the damaged cells and replace them with healthy new cells. When your body does this naturally, it improves the health of your brain. Autophagy also increases the lifespan of cells and promotes longevity.

Improves memory

Intermittent fasting also helps improve your ability to learn and retain things. Improving your memory is one of the best protective measures against neurodegenerative diseases. A diet that restricts the intake of calories helps improve your memory.

Reduces depression

Dealing with any mood disorder can be quite tricky. Medication isn't the only means to deal with such disorders. A healthy diet that doesn't fill your body with unnecessary calories leads to an overall improvement in mood. Not just mood, but it also improves your mental clarity and promotes alertness.

Chapter Four: Increased Spirituality

Thoth is believed to be the Egyptian God of magic, wisdom, writing and the moon. One of the scriptures of Thoth says, "The Soul is nourished by fire and air, and the body by water and earth."

Up until now, you were learning about the different aspects of intermittent fasting and the various benefits it offers. The increasing research in this field shows that fasting not only helps with physical healing of the body, but it has certain spiritual benefits as well. In fact, fasting has been a part of several spiritual practices since time immemorial. Fasting is not a practice that is exclusive to a single faith. There are several religions across the globe believe in the spiritual role of fasting like Christianity, Buddhism, Taoism, Islam, Jainism, Hinduism and many more.

Fasting is a healing tool that has mental, physical and spiritual benefits. It affects an individual on different plateaus of being. From a physical standpoint, fasting helps with toxin removal and helps offer protection against various diseases. From a mental and emotional standpoint, fasting helps the mind get rid of all unnecessary worries and anxieties. In fact, it also helps overcome certain addictions.

All of these benefits come together and increase exponentially when you take a look at the various spiritual benefits of fasting. Spiritual experience is something that is unique for every person. The way a person experiences the spiritual aspect of fasting differs from one person to the next. One thing that all religions agree to about fasting is that it opens up a person to form a deeper connection with his or her soul and this, in turn, makes them more receptive to forming a deeper connection with a higher power. When you focus our attention on the eternal soul that resides within, you tend to become attuned with all the energy present in the universe and the fact that this energy continuously flows within us.

By taking a break from a physical aspect of life like the consumption of food, it increases your awareness of different sensations that course through your body that you might have otherwise never noticed. The clarity of body, mind and emotions allows your spirit to come alive and it helps you realize different things about yourself, your life and the world present around you. In this section, you will learn about the spiritual symbolism of fasting in different religions and the spiritual benefits of fasting.

Fasting in Different Religions

Fasting in Christianity

In Christianity, it was believed that after John baptized Jesus in the Jordan River, Jesus had fasted for 40 days in the wilderness. The combination of these two events marks the starting point of how he started his ministry as Christ. Moses is believed to have fasted for 40 days and the same is stated in the book of Exodus. In Christianity, the purpose of a fast is to let you focus on God and not on the other materialistic things present in the world. Fasting is a means of forming and strengthening a bond with divinity and the cosmos. It is about willingly giving up your connection and attachment with the physical world of desires and concentrate on something more spiritual.

The teachings of Christianity believe that through fasting you can empower your commitment to God and your spirituality. That it helps you free yourself from the grip that Satan has over you and it opens you up for spiritual revival. It is believed that spiritual fasting helps bring you closer to the Divine being, opens you up to allow miracles into your life and sharpens your sense of spiritual awareness.

Fasting in Buddhism

According to the teachings of Buddhism, Buddha underwent an extreme fast before he received his enlightenment. Buddha believed that fasting allowed him to reach a new height of enlightenment. The scriptures show that Buddha's fast was so extreme that his eyes dug deep in his skull and he got extremely weak. It was only after he was given a bowl of porridge with milk that he accepted nourishment, and he sat in deep meditation until he attained enlightenment.

According to different Buddhist traditions, fasting is considered to be a means to reach a state of being where the mind is truly at peace regardless of any physical discomforts. In fact, it is believed to bring about inner peace even in an uncomfortable state. Buddhist teachings prescribe the importance of adopting a "middle path"- moderation of food (neither the rejection of food nor consumption in excess). Thus, the duration of the fast is flexible and it differs from one individual to the next.

Fasting in Islam

In Islam, it is believed that Muhammad initiated a method of frequent fasting and it is quite similar to the present-day method of intermittent fasting. It is believed that he used to abstain from drinking or eating anything from sunrise to sunset and did so as a means of prayer to Allah, the Almighty. In Islam, this form of fasting is quite popular during the month of Ramadan. For Muslins across the globe, this is a common method of fasting every year during the holy month of Ramadan. The fast usually lasts the entire month and is considered to be a holy offering to God.

In the Muslim faith, fasting is believed to develop self-restraint, self-discipline and a means of improving one's manners. Fasting is a spiritual shield that protects an individual from the tempting desires and sinful behaviors of the mortal world. Therefore, it produces a sense of divine equality and the freedom from want in an individual who observes the fasts. This release of the human spirit from the terrible clutches of lust and helps maintain moderation.

Fasting in Jainism

Fasting is a common practice in Jainism and it is quite similar to its eastern counterpart of Buddhism. The teachings of Jainism believe that fasting purifies the body, mind and soul of the individual and guides them on the path of asceticism and renunciation. All this is a result of the teachings of their leader - Mahavir, who spent a lot of his time fasting. According to the teachings of this faith, it is not merely about fasting, but it is about wanting to not eat. If they continue to desire food while fasting it renders the fast pointless.

In Jainism, the idea of fasting is in support to their five vows - the vow of not indulging in violence, the vow of being truthful, the vow of chastity, the vow of non-possession and the vow to not steal. The buildup of toxins in the body prevents the body from being wholesome and pure. So, they believe that fasting helps cleanse the body and mind and returns a person to their natural state of being. The teachings of Jainism are also of the opinion that fasting promotes physical healing of the body.

Fasting in Taoism

According to the religion of Taoism, fasting helps cleanse the body and mind so that a person can be a clearer state of being and have a healthy respect towards the food that nourishes the body. They believe in the simple concept of "garbage in and garbage out," if you eat food that's junk or consists of animals and plants that were mistreated, then you send your body and mind into a state of mayhem and it disrupts your natural state of being.

According to the Book of Rites, it is said that fasting also helps a person communicate with the spirit world. Fasting is associated with the chanting of religious scriptures. And it is believed that such a practice will reward the individual with good fortune that's a result of the amassing values and virtues of a pure soul. Fasting not only helps save the body from the buildup of undesirable toxins, but it also saves such a person from misfortune. Finally, fasting is also believed to make an individual conscious of his or her food consumption and this, in turn, can help the individual lead a healthy life.

"A genuine fast will cleanse the body, mind and soul. It crucifies the flesh and to that extent it helps set the soul free."- Gandhi

By now you can clearly see that spirituality and fasting go hand in hand. Fasting is an integral part of different faiths and the benefits of fasting are numerous. Ultimately, the experience that one has of fasting will be different from that of others, but a common belief is that it deepens the connection a person has with their soul and the Cosmos.

Fasting in Meditation

Fasting is not only associated with different systems of belief of faith, but it is also a major part of meditation. Deep breathing and expanding one's awareness are important proponents of meditation and fasting helps achieve all this. When your body doesn't spend energy on digesting food, your internal mechanisms adapt themselves to it and start processing nutrients from the food you consume previously. After a while, you can easily tap into the way your body feels and you can understand your body rather deeply.

It also helps you understand where different desires come from - whether a desire is a byproduct of your ego or if it is a calling from your inner soul. You become aware of all your attachments to food as a means of distraction. It allows you to take control of your spirituality and the desires of the physical world that we live in.

Deep pranamic breathing is an important part of meditation and this practice helps you gain energy. During an extended fast you can feel that your energy levels are decreasing. During such times, if you concentrate on deep breathing, you will feel refreshed and you will understand that the practice of meditation transcends the boundaries for need of food to sustain yourself.

Your intention to start a fast can be physical or spiritual. If the purpose of fasting is to promote physical healing, then you will receive it. If you fast for a spiritual reason, then you will experience the spiritual benefits as well. When you fast, you will experience all the physical, mental and spiritual benefits it offer and you will notice a positive change in your outlook towards life. You will be able to reap all these benefits along with the spiritual ones it offers.

Your body is made of muscles and organs. When you exercise you can condition your muscles.

When you fast, you can condition your body. Think of fasting as a form of exercise. It takes a while for you to condition your body and it will not happen overnight. You need to be patient with yourself and you need to give your body sufficient time to get used to the new diet.

Spiritual Benefits

Intermittent fasting is quite popular these days. After decades and decades of health fanatics proclaiming that consuming small meals throughout the day is the key to good health, now they are proclaiming the opposite of it. Limiting the intake of food is a better way to go about transforming your life for the better. In fact, with the rise in the popularity of intermittent fasting, people believe that fasting for at least 16 hours a day improves the physical and mental health of an individual.

According to experts, there are multiple reasons why intermittent fasting is good for one's health. It helps bring about mental clarity, improves the ability to concentrate, reduces the levels of sugar and improves the health of the heart. You get the idea right? There is plenty of good that comes from fasting. While all these benefits can change your life for the better. There is another aspect of fasting that needs to be given due credit and that's the effect it has on one's spirituality. As mentioned in the previous section, there are various religions that believe that fasting is a great way to open up the pathway to spiritual enlightenment.

That being said, there is so much more to fasting than not eating. So, if this concept is new to you, then here are the reasons why you need to incorporate fasting into your life to give your soul a positive nudge.

Strengthens resolve

If you are having any difficulty making a decision or are trying to understand the answer to the ever-present question of "What am I doing with my life?" then including fasting with some form of prayer will give you the answer. It will help you see past all the distractions and will strengthen your resolve. When you deny your body something, even a little bit, you are bound to be more levelheaded and will be mindful. It will put you in a better mental space that helps you get in touch with your spiritual needs and therefore, it will help you make you feel confident about the decisions that you make. Fasting helps to get rid of temptations and when you can do this, you can think better. When you can think better and in a clear manner, it certainly helps you make better decisions. Strengthening your resolve is essential to get through the hurdles of life to attain your goals.

"Fasting is a good shield for the soul, a steadfast companion for the body, a weapon for the valiant and a gymnasium for athletes."- St. Basil.

Instills discipline

Fasting requires a lot of self-discipline. Fasting is the voluntary abstinence from food. You need to discipline your mind to stop it from thinking about food when you are fasting. Selfdiscipline and self-control are often used synonymously. However, they aren't synonyms, not in the strict sense. Restraint is essential for self-discipline and self-discipline to improve self-control. Does that sound confusing? Well, it is quite simple. Only when you have a little self-control will you be able to control your impulses and not give into random whims. When you can focus and not get distracted, you can develop your selfdiscipline. If you are self-disciplined, you are bound to have a high level of self-control. So, these two concepts are dependent on one another. When you control your thoughts and impulses you can focus on the important things in life. Self-discipline is an important tool that you can use in all aspects of your life.

Humble

The world that we live in is full of distractions. In fact, most of us have the world at our fingertips and it can at times make you feel like a god. Doesn't it make you feel quite powerful that you can communicate with someone who lives across the world from you? Within a couple of swipes, you can purchase something that you want, and you can even tell others about it. Think of fasting as an antidote to all the power that we experience these days. It helps you remind about the frail nature of the human beings. After all, humans are nothing but a speck in the universe. When you remind yourself of your frailty, it helps you bring closer to God.

Closer to God

Fasting helps open up the spiritual gateway to the Cosmos. When you make a sacrifice, regardless of whether it is big or not, it brings you closer to God. It helps you connect with the cosmos on a spiritual sphere. Only when you give up something do you realize that you love something. Sacrifice, even if it's temporary, is the best way to understand what you love.

Well, if you want to reap all these spiritual benefits, then all that you need to do is get started with intermittent fasting.

Chapter Five:

Getting More Work Done

Intermittent fasting is a great way to improve your productivity. This diet not only helps improve your overall health, but it will also make you quite productivity. In this section, you will learn about the different ways in which intermittent fasting will make you productive and the simple tips that you can follow to ease the fasting period.

Become more Productive

Don't have to think about food

Regardless of whether we do it consciously or not, most of us tend to keep thinking about what the next meal will be. When you spend so much of your time thinking about what you will eat, you are essentially wasting your time. For instance, let us assume that you take about four coffee breaks while at work and each break lasts for about 15 minutes. So, you are wasting about 60 minutes of your day being absolutely unproductive. When you are fasting, you can use this time to do something else.

When you eliminate the need for food, it gives you an opportunity to be more productive. Not just that, it also helps you focus on the task at hand instead of worrying about other distractions.

Better energy levels

People tend to believe that fasting for extended periods of time will make them feel weak or even sluggish. Well, that's certainly not the case with intermittent fasting. When you are following the protocols of this diet, you condition your body to start burning its internal reserves of fat to provide energy. Once your body starts to do this, then you will have a constant supply of energy throughout the day. So, even when you don't eat, your body will keep burning fats to provide energy. Usually, you notice a sudden dip in your energy at around 4-5 in the evening. This happens because your body is used to burning glucose to provide energy and the lack of it will make you hungry. However, when you start following intermittent fasting, you will not notice any sudden dips in your energy levels and you will feel quite energetic throughout the day.

Discipline

Self-discipline is important for fasting. Selfdiscipline improves your productivity. When you know the things that you must focus on, you can get them done on time. Instead of whiling away your time on unnecessary activities, you can concentrate and improve your overall productivity. Not just that, it will even make you happy. Self-discipline ensures that you can get the right things done at the right time. All this will make you a happier individual. A person with self-discipline does have more time in a day than others. It doesn't mean that you will get extra hours in a day. It merely means that you have more time to do all the extra work when you don't procrastinate.

It helps you decide what is right and what is wrong. It helps you to distinguish between good and bad habits. Not just separate, but it even provides you the necessary willpower to do the right thing. If you get sufficient rest, nutrition, and exercise, your overall health will improve. Self-Discipline will help you in to stay healthy.

Additional Tips

Getting sufficient sleep

Getting sufficient sleep will not only keep you healthy, but will make you happier as well. The age-old saying "Early to bed, early to rise makes a man healthy, wealthy, and wise" is true. Make sure that you sleep early and get about 7-8 hours of undisturbed sleep. If you cannot wake up on your own in the morning, then you can set an alarm. Give yourself an hour to unwind before going to bed. You can read a book, watch some TV, go for a walk, or do anything that will relax you. It isn't just about the number of hours you sleep for, but the quality of sleep that matters as well. Here are a couple of simple tips that will help you in getting better sleep at night.

Set aside 8 hours for sleeping and create a sleep schedule for yourself. Go to bed and wake up at the same time every day. Try to be as consistent as possible. If you aren't able to sleep within 20 minutes of lying on the bed, leave your bedroom and do something soothing. Then go back to bed when you feel tired. After a while your body will get conditioned to the sleep schedule.

Don't get to bed when you are feeling hungry or after eating a lot. Avoid large and heavy meals before your bedtime. Physical discomfort will prevent you from sleeping. Nicotine, caffeine, and alcohol must be consumed with caution, especially before sleeping. These three substances can wreak havoc on your sleep.

Your bedroom must be cool, dark, and quiet. The room must be restful and conducive of sleeping. You cannot possibly fall asleep in a room with harsh lighting, loud music, and the wrong temperature.

If you like to take a nap during the day, try to limit it as much as you possibly can. Even when you do take a nap, don't let it exceed 30 minutes.

Develop a bedtime routine for yourself like taking a bath, reading a book, or listening to music before going to sleep. Familiarity creates a routine and there's comfort in routine.

Regular physical activity helps in sleeping better. However, don't indulge in any tiring physical activity right before going to sleep. If your body is full of adrenaline and endorphins, you won't be able to sleep.

Don't contemplate about your worries late at night. Don't let your stress get to you. Learn to manage your stress. You will learn more about this in this chapter.

Eating healthy foods

Avoid all sorts of processed foods that are full of sugars, unhealthy fats, and undesirable carbs. Instead, opt for healthy foods that are rich in fiber, nutrients and the essential macros. Healthy food will nourish your body and will leave you feeling energetic. Unhealthy foods like chocolates or chips can be replaced with some fruit or nuts. Here are a couple of simple tips that you can keep in mind to make sure that you are eating wholesome food.

Have complex carbohydrates like whole grains and leafy vegetables instead of starchy foods like bread, pasta or pizza. Your meal must be rich in protein because it not only leaves you feeling fuller for longer, but it is good for you as well. Stay away from all processed foods and instead opt for healthy treats like kale chips, nuts, fruit, or anything that isn't full of saturated fats and trans fats. Replace sugary drinks with water (sparkling or still). Create a food plan for yourself. If you are interested in cooking, then learn to experiment with recipes and cook something different. Healthy food doesn't mean bland salads, so keep an open mind and try your hand at cooking. If you plan your meals in advance, then you can do all the meal prep on your day off, this does simplify the entire cooking process.

Drink plenty of water

Water is good for your body and drinking plenty of water will make your skin clearer and will flush out all the toxins from your body. Make it a habit to have at least 8 glasses of water daily. If you want to, you can add some flavorings or electrolytes to your water to spruce it up. Slices of lemon, different berries, a handful of mint leaves, or slices of cucumber can be added to water for making detox water. By following these five simple tips, you can trick yourself into drinking water.

Drinking water needs to be convenient. Carry a water bottle or a sipper with you wherever you go. If a water bottle is handy, it is more likely that you will drink water without a reminder. Instead of sugary sodas and sweetened beverages, you can have unsweetened waterbased drinks. Instead of a Frappuccino, have a cup of Americano. Make it a point to drink a glass of water before and after your meals. Set a goal and measure the amount of water you are drinking daily. If you keep a track of your water intake, you will be motivated to drink more. Don't forget to drink water even when you go out drinking with your friends. Don't let your body get dehydrated.

Learn to manage stress

Stress can take away your happiness. You need to learn to manage stress and not let it get to you. Stress complicates things and it hinders your ability to think clearly and retards your productivity as well. Here are a couple of steps that you can follow for managing your stress.

Avoid caffeine, alcohol, and nicotine because these will just make you feel more stressed and they aren't good for your health. Caffeine and nicotine and stimulating agents, therefore they will just increase your stress instead of decreasing it. Alcohol is a depressant and too much of it will make you feel more stressed than usual

Stress increases the production of adrenaline and cortisol. These hormones are responsible for our "fight or flight" instinct. Physical exercise helps in normalizing these hormones. Not just that, physical exercise produces endorphins that will improve your overall mood and make you happier.

The importance of good sleep is paramount. You cannot function effectively and efficiently if you don't get sufficient rest. Your body needs some time to reboot its functions and recharge itself. Don't burn yourself out and give your body the rest it deserves.

You can reduce your stress by talking to someone about it. You don't have to go to a psychologist. Just talk to someone who can listen to you. When you share your stress with someone else, it does get better and a situation will not seem intimidating. You might even get a solution to solving your problem by discussing it with someone.

Stop Overeating

You need to have well-balanced meals. Eat only when you are hungry and stop yourself from eating unnecessarily. Here are a couple of simple things that you can do to avoid overeating.

Learn to eat slowly. This certainly isn't a new concept, but not many follow it. We are all in a hurry these days. Take a moment and slow down. Take a sip of water between bites and chew your food thoroughly before swallowing it. Don't just gulp your food learn to chew it slowly. **Start paying attention to what you are eating.** Savor the food you are eating and don't just stuff yourself with food. Think about the different textures and flavors. Savor every bite you eat and make it a pleasurable experience. Make your first bites count and satisfy your taste buds. **Make use of a smaller plate**, this will enable you to control the portions you eat. Stay away from foods that are rich in calories but do nothing to satisfy your appetite. Choose foods that will fill you up; foods that are satisfying. Foods rich in protein and fiber will fill your tummy. **Instead of having a bar of chocolate or a pint of ice cream, have a portion of meat with grilled vegetables.** This will satiate your hunger. Foods that are rich in calories make you feel full for a while and you will be hungry within an hour. This leads to overeating. By being mindful of what you are eating, you can stop yourself from overeating. While eating, make it a point to stay away from all electronic gadgets. This means no television. The next time you are bored, don't reach for the box of cookies or the bag of chips. Think before indulging in mindless eating.

Slow down

Did you know that it takes your brain a minimum of 20 minutes to register that you are feeling full. So, eat slowly and your brain will be able to register when you are full. You can slow down by following a very simple technique that is referred to as fork down. This will help you in enjoying your meal and eat slowly as well. It is quite simple to follow. Take smaller bites of food that you usually do and put that morsel in your mouth. Put down your fork, spoon, chopsticks or your choice of cutlery on the table and release it from your hand. Let your hands be free while you are chewing. This act of putting your fork down (quite literally) prevents you from prepping the next bite even before swallowing your last one. Now, chew your food and chew it well. Notice the texture and the taste of what you are eating. Softer food must be chewed for 5-10 times and harder or denser foods up to 30 times before you swallow it. After chewing, swallow your food completely. Once you have swallowed it, pick up your fork and reload it for your next bite. Then repeat this process all over again. Continue this technique throughout the duration of your meal. You will notice that the time spent eating will increase and you will feel fuller earlier than usual. When you feel full, stop eating. Don't eat just for the sake of eating or because there's food left.

Keep track of your weight

Start keeping a track of your weight and weigh yourself daily. This will help you in keeping a tab on your overall fitness and also assist you in identifying any changes in your weight quite easily. Your weight won't stay constant and slight fluctuations are likely. Your weight can fluctuate due to the recent meal you had, level of hydration, exercise pattern, and your menstrual cycle as well. Always weigh yourself first thing in the morning since this will provide you with a more realistic picture of your weight. You must be consistent in doing so. For all those who are tech savvy, you can track your weight by making use of several applications. There are plenty of paid and free mobile applications to choose from that will help you in keeping a track of your weight and provide you with the necessary statistics. If you are more old school, then you can maintain a diary for tracking your weight. Make it a habit to weigh yourself, but don't start obsessing about your weight. It is not just your weight that you must keep a track of, but your body measurements as well. At times, your weight might stay the same, but your measurements can differ. This will also help you in tracking your weight loss.

Eat rainbows

The best way to ensure that you have a healthy diet that provides you with all the necessary vitamins and nutrients that your body needs is by making sure that you are eating the rainbow. Yes, you read it correctly and don't take it literally. This simply means that you must include vegetables and fruit of different colors in your daily diet to improve your overall health.

Red colored foods have lycopene, an antioxidant that provides you with a burst of energy and also helps in reducing your risk of cancer. The food-list includes red peppers, tomatoes, apples, cherries, grapes, strawberries, raspberries, and watermelon. Orange colored foods contain beta-carotene (vitamin A). Foods like carrots, pumpkin, peppers, oranges, tangerines, nectarines, sweet potatoes and yams are good for your eyes. Yellow foods are rich in carotenoids and lutein that help in improving your eyesight and prevent cancer. Have a portion of yellow colored foods like peppers, cantaloupe, beans, zucchini, squash, grapefruit, lemon, and papayas. Green colored foods contain flavonoids that improve the functioning of the brain, memory, and the cardiovascular health of an individual. Have lots of green leafy vegetables and anything that's green in color. Blue and purple colored foods also have flavonoids and include blueberries, nightshades like eggplant and peppers, red cabbage and grapes. White colored foods like cauliflower, garlic, peas, potatoes, bananas, and pears contain selenium and allicin that are good for the heart.

Keeping your portions in check

You must start keeping a track of the portions you eat. This will also help in making sure that you are having a well-balanced meal. Your calorie intake must be less than the calories you are burning. If it isn't, then your body will simply start storing the remaining calories in the form of fat cells and you will gain weight. You don't need a set of measuring cups and a measuring scale for keeping an eye on the portions you consume. You can measure the portions by using your hand. Yes, it is quite simple and regardless of where you are, you will always be able to check the portion size.

As a rule of thumb, men will need two portions and women will need just one. Your palm signifies the amount of protein you must eat. The recommended amount of meat in a meal is about 3 ounces or the size and weight of a deck of cards. Your palm without including your fingers is close to this size. The amount of vegetable that you must include in a meal is equivalent to your clenched fist. Now, cup your hand and that's the amount of carbs that you must have in a meal. Carbs can be obtained from pastas, breads, and even starchy veg like potatoes. Fats must be equivalent to the size of your thumb. That's approximately the size of a tablespoon. For measuring the portion of cheese, make use of your fingers. A portion of cheese must be roughly equivalent to two of your fingers placed together.

So, to sum it all up, a piece of meat that fits into your palm, a fistful of vegetables, a cupped hand of carbs, your thumb represents the portion of fat and your fingers for the portion of cheese. If you have three to four meals a day by making use of the above-mentioned portions, then you will be having a wellbalanced meal.

Chapter Six: Success Stories

A good diet is all that you need to turn your life around. You don't need powerful and expensive medicines to better your life. You merely need to be mindful of what you eat and when you eat, and Janielle Wright's story will reinforce this belief.

Janielle Wright is a health and a beauty influencer who weighed 337 lbs. before following the protocols of intermittent fasting. Her body used to be in constant pain and she even had trouble breathing at night. She used to go to sleep worrying that she might not wake up in the morning. Her worries weren't restricted to her health, the 28-year old mother was worried that she will never get to see her daughter, Noah, grow up. She was tired of all the fad diets that promised quick results. All such diets did her no good and only made it worse for her health. In January 2018, she decided to try intermittent fasting. By restricting her eating window and eating only during the feeding window, she managed to lose over 65 pounds.

Wright chose a method of intermittent fasting that restricted her eating window to about 8 hours and she was essentially fasting for the other 16 hours. She scheduled her diet such that her first meal was at noon and her last meal at around 8 p.m. She was eating only two meals per day and was avoiding snacking between her meals. She stuck to low-carb meals and her daily calorie intake was between
1800 to 2000 calories per day. She used MyFitnessPal app to track her calorie intake.

She wanted to change, and she wanted to do something to not just lose weight but improve her overall health as well. Intermittent fasting addressed all her concerns and really helped her turn her life around.

The one thing about intermittent fasting that Wright enjoys is the fact that it doesn't place any restrictions on the kind of foods you can, as long as you avoid junk food. A consistent exercise routine and piously following the diet helped her drop over 65 pounds in less than six months. About 15 minutes of warm-up cardio and 30 minutes of intensive exercising six days a week helped speed up her weight loss. She says consistency is the key. She loved her experience with intermittent fasting so much that she believes she can sustain her new diet even in the long run. Being constant, consistent and patient are the three things she believes helped her achieve her weight loss and fitness goals.

If she can do it, then so can you!

If Wright's store inspired you, here is another story that will certainly want you to get started with your diet today!

Dwayne managed to drop 52 lbs. in seven months. He is just like you, a normal guy, with a happy family, who likes his work and is happy in general. Everything was great in his life except for the fact that he was overweight and needed a good diet that will help him lose weight in a healthy manner. While looking for the "perfect" diet, he stumbled across intermittent fasting and there was no looking back for him since then. Dwayne claims that following the diet for seven months has made him feel like he is a new person altogether. The diet has made him change his unhealthy eating habits and has helped him lead a healthier life. He claims that intermittent fasting coupled with nutritious meals and a little exercise have helped him not only lose weight but make him feel quite energetic as well. Apart from this, the diet has also improved his mental clarity and overall productivity.

Intermittent fasting is also quite popular among Hollywood celebrities. Several celebrities like Hugh Jackman, Terry Crews, Beyoncé, Jennifer Lopez, Nicole Kidman and Ben Affleck swear by this diet. So, if you want to look like your favorite celebrity, then all that you need to do is start following the diet that helps them retain their good

Conclusion

I want to thank you once again for purchasing this book. I hope it proved to be an entertaining and an informative read.

Intermittent fasting is a wonderful diet that is quite different from all the traditional diets. It is quite simple to follow this dynamic diet. You merely need to select an eating window for yourself and you are good to go. As long as you eat only during the eating window and fast throughout the day, you will be able to see a positive change in your life within no time. While following this diet, you need to be patient with yourself and keep an open mind.

Now, that you are aware of all the different aspects of this diet along with the benefits it offers, the next step is to get started as soon as you can. If you are ready to turn your life around and achieve your weight loss and fitness goals, then OMAD is the diet for you! So, go ahead, take the first step to turning your life around!

Thank you and all the best!

Resources

https://www.healthline.com/nutrition/intermittent-fasting-and-weight-loss

https://blog.bulletproof.com/intermittentfasting-benefits/

http://grottonetwork.com/keep-thefaith/belief/spiritual-benefits-of-intermittentfasting/

https://www.thriveglobal.com/stories/howfasting-absolutely-skyrocketed-myproductivity/

https://www.dietdoctor.com/intermittentfasting/success-stories/all